Sorry, I Love You ...

A play

John Goodrum

Samuel French — London
New York - Toronto - Hollywood

SORRY, I LOVE YOU ...

First produced by Rumpus Theatre Company at the Quay
Theatre, Sudbury, on 27th October 2001 as part of a
national tour with the following cast:

Helen	Susan Earnshaw
The Tramp	Nick Wyatt
Jools	Oliver Hume

Directed by John Goodrum
Designed by John B. Scattergood
Lighting by Keith Tuttle
Sound recording and design by David Gilbrook

COPYRIGHT INFORMATION

(See also page ii)

CHARACTERS

Helen: thirties
Jools: thirties
Tramp
Costos
Airport Check-In Man
Stewardess
Irish Hotel Receptionist
American Hotel Receptionist played by the same
Japanese Hotel Receptionist actor
Russian Hotel Receptionist
Pizza Delivery Man
Voice of DJ
Ageing Playboy
Zoo-Keeper
Voice of Pete: recorded

The action of the play takes place on a street in Wimbledon; in a café; in the Heathrow check-in lounge; in an aeroplane; in the reception areas and bedrooms of hotels in Cork, Los Angeles, Tokyo and Moscow; on a cliff in Cork and a bridge in Moscow; a flat; a nightclub; and a zoo.

Time — Present

AUTHOR'S NOTE

Pop music is the backdrop to this play and in the script I have specified the music we used in the first production. Future directors should feel free to choose music of their own, but it should be relevant to each particular stage of the story and should include some tracks that are very contemporary.

My thanks are due to all those involved in the first production, and to my father for his constant and invaluable support.

John Goodrum

ACT 1
Scene 1

A street in Wimbledon. (For set suggestions, see p.57) Late afternoon. Winter

Helen (*shouting; off*) Look. This is me. I'm leaving. Now.

Helen enters carrying a barely closed, badly packed suitcase and several hastily gathered personal possessions, including a teddy, tapes, clothes and books

(*Yelling to a point off stage and high above her*) Goodbye forever! I hope!
Pete (*distantly; off*) What about the CD player?
Helen (*yelling as before*) Oh ... Keep the bloody CD player!
Pete (*distantly; off*) I don't want your bloody CD player! You bought it! You have it! Here!

There is the sound of expensive electronic equipment being dropped down several storeys on to a concrete floor

And here's all your CDs to go with it.

There is the sound of a succession of CDs being hurled down with some vehemence

Helen (*to herself*) Oh ... (*She pauses*) Bugger. (*She sits on the pavement*)

The Nat King Cole version of "Let There Be Love" *plays*

Helen looks ruefully at the scatter of possessions lying about her, then notices something that reminds her of some happy memory. She picks it up and turns it over in her hands, smiling. Then some bad memory strikes her and she drops whatever it is she has picked up and throws a black look in Pete's direction. She repacks her case

When she has nearly finished her packing, the music fades out

The Tramp enters and makes to walk past, but sees Helen on the pavement and stops

Tramp (*Cockney*) Spare a couple of quid, miss?
Helen Shouldn't I be asking you that?
Tramp What?
Helen Well ... (*She indicates that she is sitting on the pavement*)

Tramp (*getting the joke*) Oh ... yeah. Yeah, I see what you mean.
Helen You can have a CD player if you'd like it.
Tramp A CD player?
Helen To play CDs on.
Tramp Oh no, no. That'd be no good to me. I don't 'ave the electric, you see.
Helen Ah. Yes. Probably wouldn't work anyway.
Tramp No. A couple of quid'd be better. I could get a cup of tea and a
    sandwich with that.
Helen Right.
Tramp There's a café just round the corner.
Helen Sounds good.

Helen finds her purse and gives the Tramp a couple of coins

    Here you are.
Tramp Thanks, miss. (*He walks away in the direction he was going, but
    when he's just past Helen he turns back*) Be lucky. (*He turns to leave*)

    Jools enters, in a hurry, from the direction in which the Tramp is heading

The Tramp bumps into Jools

Jools Oh ...
Tramp Spare a couple of quid, sir?
Jools Ah ... I'm afraid I — er ...
Tramp Never mind, sir. Thanks, sir. Be lucky.

    The Tramp exits

Jools sees Helen sitting on the pavement

Jools Oh.

Helen doesn't notice Jools

    Um ...
Helen (*looking up*) What?
Jools Er ...
Helen (*liking what she sees*) Oh!

Helen and Jools look at each other for a few moments

    Hallo.

Jools Er … hallo.

Pause

    Um … Is this — er … Is this Richmond Street?
Helen Yes. Yes it is.
Jools I'm — um … I'm looking for number fifty-two.
Helen (*a little deflated*) Oh. Are you?
Jools Yes. Er … flat three.
Helen (*flatly*) Flat three.
Jools Yes. Flat three, fifty-two Richmond Street.
Helen (*coldly*) Well, up you go, then.
Jools Up I go?
Helen He's waiting for you.
Jools Waiting for me?
Helen Pete.
Jools Oh, yes. Pete.
Helen You are Jools, aren't you?
Jools Well — Yes … Julian, really.
Helen (*mocking*) Oh, "Julian".
Jools Jools to my friends.
Helen Go on, "Julian". Your friend's waiting for you upstairs.
Jools Oh, my God! You're not …
Helen What?
Jools Are you … ?
Helen How do you do. My name's Helen.
Jools Oh, my God! You are! Look, can I … ?
Helen What?
Jools Do you need a hand — with — all … ? (*He gestures vaguely towards the things surrounding Helen*)
Helen "All" … ? (*She realizes what Jools means*) Oh! No. No, I'm fine. I regularly sit in the gutter surrounded by a few badly packed treasured possessions.
Jools It's very cold.
Helen I'm fine.
Jools Middle of winter.
Helen I've got my thermals on. You go up and comfort poor old Pete.
Jools Yes … Well — difficult time.
Helen It is.
Jools I'm his oldest friend.
Helen Are you? I've never seen you before.
Jools No.
Helen How long've Pete and I been together?

Jools Five years.
Helen Five years, yes. (*Indignantly*) How do you know?
Jools I'm his oldest friend.
Helen He's hardly mentioned you. Only to say he was calling you today.
Jools Well, I live in Finsbury Park, actually.
Helen Do you?
Jools It's a bit of a long way.
Helen We're only in Wimbledon!
Jools I hate travelling.
Helen First time in five years, just to cross London! Not much of a best friend.
Jools Yes — well — friendships tend to take a bit of a back seat, don't they?
     When you're with someone.
Helen Do they?
Jools I think so. Yes.

Pause

     Well — if you're sure?
Helen Oh, yes. You just hop back into the front seat, put on your safety belt
     and have a good old chat about old times with Pete.
Jools Lovely.

Pause

     What are you going to do now?
Helen Me? Oh, I don't know.
Jools Ah.
Helen Yes, I do.
Jools Oh?
Helen There's a café just round the corner. I'm going to have a cup of tea.
     And a sandwich.
Jools Well done. Keep your strength up!

Pause. Jools hovers

Helen Goodbye, then.
Jools Oh ... Yes — goodbye.

Jools hovers for a few moments. He makes to go into the building, but then turns to Helen

     Goodbye.
Helen Goodbye.

Jools hovers a second more and then exits into the building

(*Looking after Jools; appreciatively*) Mmm!

The Jay Kay/Jools Holland version of "I'm in the Mood for Love" plays

Helen gathers her belongings up and exits the way the Tramp exited

The Lights cross-fade to the next scene

SCENE 2

The Café. Early evening

Costos (played by the same actor who played the Tramp) enters and sets up the café. (See p.57) A table and chairs are set up; there are a grubby menu, an ashtray, a salt cellar and a vinegar bottle on the table. When he has finished, he exits

Helen enters the café. She looks around for a spare table. She finds one, sits down, and waits, trying to make out the menu

The music fades

The Lights flicker and go out

Costos (*shouting in a strong Greek accent; off*) Bloody fuse box!

The Lights come on again with a flicker

Costos enters with a tea towel in his hand. He heads towards Helen

(*Shouting back to someone*) We get someone tomorrow. I tell you, it needs fixing. (*To Helen, surly*) Whaddaya want?
Helen Well …
Costos You have to drink, yeah?
Helen Yes, please, I'll have a cup of — —
Costos Coffee, yeah?
Helen No. A cup of tea, please.
Costos (*suspiciously*) Oh yeah? You want to eat?
Helen Yes. What sandwiches do you do?
Costos Sandwich?
Helen Yes.
Costos (*going*) Sandwich.

Helen (*calling after him*) No. What sandwiches do you … ?
Costos (*shouting to someone off stage*) Sandwich!

Costos exits

Helen Oh. Pot luck then.

The Lights flicker and go off again

Costos (*shouting; off*) Bloody thing!

> *The Tramp* (*played by the same actor who played Costos*) *enters in the darkness carrying a sandwich on a plate and a mug of tea. He sits opposite Helen and puts the plate and mug on the table*

The Lights come on again with a flicker

Tramp (*recognizing Helen*) 'Allo, miss!
Helen (*surprised, recognizing the Tramp*) Oh! Hallo.
Tramp I didn't see you come in.
Helen (*puzzled, looking around her*) No … er …
Tramp I got me sandwich.
Helen (*settling herself*) I'm pleased. What is it?
Tramp I dunno. I ordered cheese and 'am.
Helen Isn't it cheese and ham?
Tramp I don't think so. It smells like fish.
Helen Probably is fish, then.
Tramp (*examining his sandwich*) I think you're right. It *is* fish.
Helen Why don't you send it back?
Tramp Oh no! I don't want to upset Costos. 'E might ban me.
Helen Would that be so terrible?
Tramp Bloody 'ell, it would! I don't want to miss out on food as good as this!
  (*He eats the sandwich during the following*)

Pause

Helen (*holding out her hand to the Tramp*) My name's Helen. Helen Richards. How do you do.

The Tramp wipes his hand on his coat and holds it out

Tramp 'Ow do ya do, miss.
Helen (*shaking his hand*) Do you — have a name?

Tramp I should think so, miss, but it's been so long since somebody called me by it I can't rightly remember. Albert rings a bell — but then again that could've been my dad. Seems the sort of name 'e should've 'ad some'ow.

Helen smiles

Pause

Audrey rings a bell.
Helen (*with a wry smile*) That's not you, is it?
Tramp Oh, no! I know 'oo Audrey is. She's my wife. Well … She *was* — up until she walked out on me.
Helen (*slightly embarrassed*) Oh … I'm sorry.
Tramp That's all right. I expect I deserved it. No, it's just that things've gone a bit 'aywire since she left. I can't seem to make 'ead or tail of anything much.
Helen How long ago did she leave you?
Tramp Well, that's one of the things that's gone, to be honest wiv yer. It could've been six years ago … It could've been yesterday. I don't know. (*He looks at his hands*) Me 'ands look older than they did when I was with 'er, so it must've been a bit of a while, I suppose.

Pause

Helen Actually — I've just walked out on someone.
Tramp 'Ave yer, miss?
Helen Well, I say "walked out". I'm not sure if I walked or if I was thrown.
Tramp Cor! Big row, was it?
Helen Lots of them. Lots of big rows. And two very unhappy people. In the end he said, "All right then, go!" And I said, "Don't worry, I will!"
Tramp Mutual, then.
Helen Yes … Very good … "Mutual".
Tramp Worth another try, d'you think?
Helen No … No, there've been lots of tries. No more tries, please.
Tramp Best get on with it, then. Forget all about 'im and start over.
Helen Yes.

Pause

Tramp What'll 'appen to 'im, d'you think? This bloke you've just walked out on. Will 'e forget 'is name and end up like me?
Helen (*meaning it*) Oh, no. No, I don't think so.
Tramp Good on 'im! And you'll be OK, won't yer? Nice young girl like you.

Helen Not so young now.

Tramp Not so old neever! (*Neither*) Yeah! You'll soon find someone else you fancy.

Helen Maybe. (*She half laughs, remembering Jools*)

Tramp Oh? You 'ave already, 'ave you? Blimey, you're a quick worker! What didya do? Meet 'im on the steps as you walked out?

Helen Well ...

Tramp (*thinking for a moment*) 'Ang on. You 'aven't fallen for me, 'ave you?

Helen Oh ...

Tramp Blimey! Don't fall for me. I'm an 'undred an' five years old and I ain't got no money. You can do better for yourself than that.

Helen No. No, I'm sorry. It wasn't you.

Tramp Don't be sorry, miss. You just done yourself a favour! (*Realization dawning*) Oh, I know! It's Mr — er — er — um, innit? Oh, well. 'E's nice enough looking, I suppose.

Helen If you mean who I think you mean, I don't "fancy" him. And anyway, he's a friend of Pete's.

Tramp (*knowingly*) Is 'e? (*Pause*) 'Oo's Pete?

Helen The man I've just walked out on.

Tramp Oh. I see.

Helen (*more for her own sake than for the Tramp's*) But that doesn't automatically make him a villain, does it? I mean — *I* was a friend of Pete's too, once, wasn't I? I was a special friend. No. He's probably not so bad as all that, this Jools.

Tramp (*incredulous*) Is that 'is name?

Helen What?

Tramp "Jools"?

Helen Oh, yes — Jools.

Tramp 'E sounds like a right ponce! Still, if you fancy 'im, I suppose.

Helen I don't fancy him! I don't know anything about him! I'll probably never ever see him again.

Tramp Oh, I dunno. Tell you what, I'm a bit of a gypsy, now, ain't I? Why don't I try and work a bit of magic, eh? Weave a little spell? See if I can do something about it.

Helen (*laughing*) I don't know that I *want* to see him again.

Tramp No! Let me try. Go on. Just a bit of fun. 'Ere goes. (*Waving his hands around and chanting in a silly voice*) Ooh! Ooh! Jools! Jools! Come on, mate. Come to 'Elen! (*Returning to his normal voice*) There you are. That should do it!

Helen (*laughing*) You're mad!

Tramp It's being on me own so much that does it. (*Getting up, having finished his sandwich*) Well, it's been very nice talking with you, miss. Thanks for sparing me the time. And for the sandwich too, of course. I must go now. I've got an appointment with a solicitor — got to sort out me divorce papers. Or was that six years ago? … Be lucky, girl. (*Meaning it*) Go for it!

The Tramp exits

Helen smiles, almost laughs

Helen (*remembering her tea and sandwich*) Oh! (*She looks over her shoulder*)

Jools enters from the side of the stage opposite Helen. He sees Helen and comes up to her

Jools Er … Hallo.
Helen (*jumping and turning back*) Good God! Hallo! … It worked!
Jools What worked?
Helen Oh — nothing.
Jools Er … Can I join you?
Helen What are you doing here?
Jools Well …
Helen Shouldn't you be with Pete? Isn't that why you came over?
Jools I *was* with Pete. In the pub — the *Nelson* — down the road, you know? Well, of course you do. You live here, don't you … ? Well — you *did*. I mean … Oh, sorry …
Helen What are you doing here?
Jools I — just — suddenly felt hungry — for no reason — a couple of minutes ago. And the pub didn't do any food. Well, only crisps and stuff. So the barman told me about this place.
Helen The barman?
Jools He recommended it.
Helen What about Pete? Wasn't he hungry?
Jools Ah — no — he'd already eaten, you see.
Helen Had he?
Jools Yes. Fish and chips. Just after you left … Oh.
Helen He's not suffering *too* much then.
Jools Well — inside I think.
Helen Where did he get these fish and chips from?
Jools Oh, some place — just along from the flat … Do you know it?
Helen I know it. He *will* be suffering inside.
Jools Can I sit down?
Helen If you want to.
Jools Thanks.

Jools sits opposite Helen

   (*Picking up the menu*) Have you ordered?
Helen Yes. (*Looking over her shoulder*) I don't know what's happened to
   it.
Jools (*looking at the counter*) Should I go up myself, do you think?
Helen If you like. Ask them about my sandwich.
Jools Does it usually take as long as this?
Helen I don't know. I've never been here before.
Jools Oh. I thought you were a regular.
Helen Me? No.
Jools Oh.
Helen Well, you don't, do you? When you live just round the corner.
Jools (*getting up*) I think I will go up.

Costos enters with Helen's sandwich, her cutlery and a napkin

Costos I come! I come!

Jools sits down again, cowed

(*Slamming the sandwich down in front of Helen*) Here! Your coffee comes
in a minute.
Helen Tea.
Costos (*to Jools*) Whaddaya want?
Jools Er ...
Costos You have to drink, yeah?
Jools Well ...
Costos Coffee, yeah?
Jools Er ... OK.
Costos You want to eat?
Jools Yes. (*Looking at the menu*) I'll have ... Er ...
Costos What?
Jools I'll have ...
Costos You want a sandwich?
Jools No. I'll ... Um ...
Costos You don't want a sandwich?
Jools No, thanks. I'll have a cheese omelette and chips.
Costos (*suspiciously*) Cheese omelette and chips?
Jools Yes, please.
Costos You want peas or beans with that?
Jools Er ...
Costos Beans. Right.

Jools Er ... No ...

Costos (*turning to go*) Cheese omelette, chips and beans.

Jools But ...

Costos (*heading towards the exit, shouting off*) Cheese omelette, chips and beans!

Costos exits

Jools I hate baked beans! ... (*Quietly, jokingly*) Help.

Helen is amused

How's your sandwich?

Helen It's actually very good. It's chicken. I wouldn't've chosen chicken but it *is* chicken and it's very good. He was right.

Jools Who was?

Helen The tramp. He was here a minute ago.

Jools What tramp?

Helen You met him outside the flat.

Jools Did I?

Helen You can't've forgotten.

Jools I forget everything.

Pause. Helen eats

Helen Look, I don't know what Pete's told you about me, but ... Well — I'm actually quite a nice person, really. I wasn't nice when I was with Pete. But — well — *he* wasn't very nice then, either. Maybe it's just *us* that weren't nice. Us together, I mean. As a couple. We're both perfectly nice people on our own ... I think.

Jools Oh, I know *Pete's* a nice person. He's great. (*He suddenly realizes his rudeness. Trying too hard*) And I'm sure *you* are, too. Very nice. As nice as it's possible to be. Wonderful.

There is a slight pause

Pete's got his faults, of course. But — then again — haven't we all! He used to annoy the hell out of me at university. We'd be late for a lecture and he still wouldn't walk fast. He'd just dawdle. Walk even slower, on purpose. In the end I'd just leave him and hurry on. But by then it'd be too late, of course, and I'd be late anyway.

Helen He still does that.

Jools Does he?

Helen I've not seen the beginning of a film for the last five years. It doesn't matter how early I try to get him started, we're still always late. *Were*, I mean. *Were* always late.

Jools He's good fun, though. No one better to have round to dinner.

Helen Oh, no. In the beginning we used to spend all our time laughing. He could keep me going for hours. Just when I thought I was calming down he'd say something else and I'd be off again, helpless.

There is a pause. Helen, remembering, nearly cries

Jools I think you're perfectly nice.

Costos enters with a Coke

Costos (*giving the Coke to Helen*) Here. (*He heads for the exit*)
Helen This is a Coke.
Costos (*leaving*) I know. I just brought it.

Costos exits

Helen Do you think you ever get the right food in this place?
Jools I hope not.
Helen Is that where you and Pete met? At university?
Jools (*nodding*) We just sort of found ourselves together, really. Doing the same course. Then we used to see each other quite a lot after we left. Then less so. Sometimes only once or twice a year. Then, when I got married — —
Helen (*involuntarily*) Oh!
Jools What?
Helen You're married?
Jools Well ... Yes ...
Helen Ah.
Jools Just.
Helen Just?
Jools I'm sort of a bit married.
Helen Can you do it by degrees? I thought you were either married or you weren't.
Jools Well, I *am* married — technically. That is to say, I'm not divorced — yet. But we're not together — at the moment — at all. And not likely to be — ever again. Besides, I live in Finsbury Park and she lives in Brixton.
Helen (*mockingly*) Oh, miles apart!
Jools (*seriously*) Exactly. So ...
Helen Why did you split up?

Jools Oh, one reason mainly.

Helen What's that?

Jools She hates me.

Helen Ah.

Jools Well ... Maybe not *me* so much as the job I do. Or, rather, the fact that I *do* it — all the time — rather obsessively — or so she said.

Helen What is this job?

Jools I make toys.

Helen (*interestedly*) Do you?

Jools Well ... No — I don't actually *make* them ... Well — not *lots* of them. I invent them. I invent toys. For other people to mass produce. (*He digs a small toy out of his pocket and holds it out to Helen*) Here, look at this.

Helen (*taking the toy*) What is it?

Jools It's a cyber baby. You have to love it, feed it, change it, take it to the park. Every few hours.

Helen How do you feed an electronic toy?

Jools You press this button on the side here (*he does so*) and it comes up with a menu of options. "Feed" is number two.

Helen Right.

Jools If it wants something it cries. There's a different cry for each thing it wants. It's up to you to work out which cry is which yourself.

Helen How many options are there?

Jools Forty-five. The last one is "Wipe bottom" .

Helen What's the point of it?

Jools Well, every now and then — if you want to — you can press this button on the other side here and it'll tell you what sort of a parent you are. Go on. Press it. See how good I am.

Helen (*reading from the toy*) "Taken into care." Oh God, that's terrible.

Jools It's not the worst.

Helen Isn't it?

Jools Top of the tree is "Super Dad".

Helen How does it know you're a dad?

Jools You have to register, when you first turn it on. Next best is "Good Dad". Then it goes "OK Dad"; then "Staying with grandparents for the weekend"; "Staying with grandparents for the week"; "Staying with grandparents for the month"; "Staying with grandparents"; "Taken into care" and "Dead". If it reaches "Dead" it just turns itself off.

Helen And you invented this?

Jools Yes.

Helen It's horrible!

Jools Thanks. The more grotesque it is, the better it'll sell. You can have that one if you like.

Helen What?

Jools I've got loads of them at home. All different prototypes. That's not the latest.

Helen I don't want it. It'll call me Dad.

Jools Try it out. See how it feels.

Helen I can't look after this all the time. I'm not the sort. It'll die.

Jools It doesn't matter. If it dies, you just reset it with this button and start again. See how you get on. She's called Melanie.

Helen looks at the toy

Helen Easier than a real baby.

Jools Yes.

Pause

Since I seem to be telling you all about myself, you might as well know, I've got loads of *them* as well.

Helen What? Loads of real babies?

Jools Yes — well — two, actually. Twins. And they're not babies any more. They're four. And eleven months. And two weeks.

Helen What are their names?

Jools Stephen James and Amelia Ruth. Emmy. They live with my — well — Jane — my — ex — well — soon-to-be ex-wife, in Brixton. But I see them every week — most weeks — nothing formal, just arranged between us. She's happy for me to see them. Either I go over there or she drops them over to me. It's a bit of a pain, really. Finsbury Park and Brixton. I don't drive, you see. Never have done.

Helen Is that where you used to live? Brixton?

Jools Mm. Not my house any more, of course. She bought me out. So I could buy the flat. In Finsbury Park.

Helen Why didn't you buy a flat in Brixton?

Jools Well ... At the time — last year — I wanted a bit of distance. Didn't want to be on top of her — as it were. Wanted to be out of the way — you know — if she wanted to — well ...

Pause

Helen (*wanting to know*) How about now? Would you like to be on top of her now?

Jools No. No, she's right. I got so involved in all this work that we grew apart. To be honest, we were never that much good as lovers in the first place. It was exciting for a while, but ... No, all that's gone. We get on much better

now we're apart. It's good — for the kids. (*Looking around*) Is there a loo
here? I'm desperate after all that beer.
Helen I've no idea.
Jools Yes. I think there's one over there. I won't be a moment.
Helen OK.

Jools exits in search of the loo

Helen eats her sandwich

*Costos enters with a plate of cheese salad, a glass of milk, cutlery and
napkin*

Costos (*to Helen*) He's gone?
Helen Yes ... I mean — he's coming back.

Costos bangs the plate and glass down in Jools' place and turns to go

Helen (*bravely*) Er ... excuse me ...
Costos (*turning back, threateningly*) You speak?
Helen Er ... Yes.
Costos Whaddaya want?
Helen It's just that I think my friend ordered an omelette, not a salad.
Costos (*indicating the salad*) He likes that.
Helen Does he?
Costos He likes that.
Helen Oh. Right.
Costos You like him?
Helen What?
Costos This man — you like him?
Helen (*disarmed*) Oh ... Yes ... But ...
Costos But what?
Helen He's married.
Costos (*with a shrug*) Pfff! He's not married.
Helen Yes, he is.
Costos He's not married. He likes you. I know.
Helen You're not related to that tramp who was here just now, are you?
Costos "Tramp"? What is "tramp"? I don't know "tramp" ...

Jools comes back from the loo

Costos (*to Jools*) You live with someone who's your wife?
Jools What?
Costos You live with someone who's your wife?

Jools Well ... No ... No, I don't.

Costos (*to Helen*) I tell you. Be happy. (*To them both*) Enjoy your food. (*He heads for the exit, calling angrily to someone off stage*) Yes, yes! I come. I come.

Costos exits

Jools (*seeing the salad and the milk*) Oh.

Helen He says you'll like it.

Jools No beans, anyway. (*He starts to eat*)

Pause

Helen How is it?

Jools (*his mouth full*) Excellent.

Helen It's amazing! He seems to see through what you order to what you'd really like. Don't you have that? When you're in a restaurant — or a café or whatever — looking at the menu, you order what you *think* you'd like, rather than what you really *would* like. I do that all the time. I'm often disappointed.

Jools Me too. (*He reaches for the salt*) Excuse me.

Helen (*picking up the salt cellar to hand it to Jools*) No, here ...

They find themselves both holding the salt cellar, therefore each other's hands

Jools (*letting go, embarrassed*) Oh.

Helen (*also letting go, embarrassed*) Sorry.

Jools No.

Suddenly there is a loud electronic crying

Helen (*jumping*) Dear God! What's that?

Jools It's Melanie.

Helen Melanie?

Jools Your new baby.

Helen Oh — Lord! (*Picking up the doll*) Well, come on, then! What the hell does *this* cry mean?

Jools As you've only just got it, I'll help you out. That's an "I want my teddy" cry.

Helen (*fiddling with the buttons*) Oh. Right.

Jools I'm getting to know them all.

Helen Didn't you invent them?

Jools I know, but ...

Helen (*pushing a button*) There.

The crying stops

There is a slight pause

Jools Seriously — what *are* you going to do now?
Helen Oh … I don't know.
Jools I mean, where are you going to live?
Helen Live?
Jools What's your job? I don't know anything about you. (*A slight pause*) I've told you all about *me*. It's only fair.

There is a slight pause

Helen Well … I suppose I shall have to find a flat — unless I go back to live with Mother.
Jools Where does your mother live?
Helen Lewisham.
Jools (*wisely*) Find a flat. Can you pay for it?
Helen Yes.
Jools Do you have a job?
Helen Yes!
Jools What is it?
Helen I'm a — a freelance journalist.
Jools Are you?
Helen Yes.
Jools Freelance?
Helen All right! I'm an *unemployed* journalist! Or — at any rate — I'm between contracts at the moment. I finished a very lucrative one a couple of months ago and I've still living off that.
Jools Come to Ireland with me.
Helen (*taken aback*) What?
Jools Come to Ireland with me.
Helen (*amazed*) Ireland?
Jools Yes.
Helen Why Ireland?
Jools I'm going there tomorrow.
Helen I thought you hated travelling.
Jools I do. But I have to go. For my job.
Helen Why?
Jools To promote my new toy. Not the cyber baby. The one before that. The one that's going on the market this week. I have to do a tour of international toy fairs. Starting tomorrow. In Cork.

Helen Cork?

Jools Then Los Angeles. Then Tokyo. Then Moscow ...

Helen And where then?

Jools Finsbury Park. The tour ends in Moscow.

Helen Are you asking me out on a date? Or is it a dirty weekend you've got in mind?

Jools Neither ... I don't know. Come to Ireland with me. It's all free. The company pays for everything. You see, I'm allowed to take a partner — and — well — now that Jane doesn't come any more the ticket's going begging.

Helen Jools ...

Jools Separate rooms, of course. I'm not suggesting anything. (*A slight pause*) It would just be nice.

Pause

Helen Won't you be busy? With your new toy?

Jools Three hours in the morning, the day after tomorrow. We'd have all tomorrow evening and all the next afternoon and evening, before I'd have to fly on to America on Sunday.

Helen Jools ... I have to find somewhere to live.

Jools Do all that when you come back. You can stay over in Finsbury Park tonight.

Helen I'm your best friend's girlfriend.

Jools (*without any inflection*) I thought you weren't any more. I thought that was why I came over?

There is a slight pause

Helen I won't come as your token partner.

Jools I'm not asking you to.

Pause

Helen I'm going to find a hotel tonight. Stay there.

Pause

Jools The flight leaves at two twenty. Think about it. Please.

Pause

(*Suddenly remembering*) Oh!

Helen What?
Jools Pete!
Helen Pete?
Jools I said I'd go back — after I'd eaten.
Helen Go back?
Jools He's waiting.
Helen Oh.
Jools In the pub.
Helen Right.

There is a slight pause

Jools I did promise.
Helen Yes. Of course.
Jools (*feeling in his pockets*) Best not to take sides.
Helen No.
Jools (*in sudden realization*) Oh!

There is a slight pause

Helen What?
Jools I haven't got any money.
Helen What?
Jools The little bit I had on me went on drinks in the pub.

There is a slight pause

Helen Well … Haven't you got a cashpoint card?
Jools Oh … Yes.
Helen There you are, then. I'll tell them you're coming back.
Jools OK … Only — it's at home. I think.
Helen At home.
Jools Yes.
Helen Right.
Jools So …

Pause

Jools Um — I don't suppose you could … ?
Helen What?
Jools Just till tomorrow …
Helen Jools!
Jools I'll pay you back at the airport.

Helen I'm not coming to the airport!
Jools You'd have to come then — —
Helen OK. I'll pay for you.
Jools — to get your money back.
Helen I'll pay for you!
Jools (*getting up*) Thanks. Don't forget — two-twenty.
Helen I'm not coming.
Jools No. Of course not!
Helen I'm not coming.
Jools (*heading for the exit*) I heard you.
Helen (*just stopping Jools before he exits*) Jools?
Jools (*turning back*) What?

They look at each other for a moment

Helen Which airport?
Jools (*smiling*) Heathrow. Terminal one. Bye.

Jools exits

Helen (*calling after Jools*) I'm not coming! (*She looks at the door where Jools has exited*)

The Lights go out

Costos (*shouting; off*) Bloody fuse box!

The Lights come on again with a flicker

Helen smiles, still looking at the door

"Kiss Me" by Sixpence None The Richer plays

Helen indicates for Costos to come over to her

Costos enters. He comes up to Helen. In dumb show she asks how much the two meals were and pays Costos

Helen picks up her case and exits

Costos gathers up the plates and glass and exits

The Lights cross-fade to the next scene

SCENE 3

Heathrow check-in lounge. Early afternoon

Jools enters with a case

Jools sets up the Heathrow check-in desk and scales. (See p.58) Then he stands and waits, with his case beside him, anxiously looking at his watch

The music fades

Tannoy Will passengers for Aer Lingus flight EI oh-seven-one-five to Cork please proceed to gate seventeen where the flight is now boarding. Passengers for Aer Lingus flight EI oh-seven-one-five to Cork please proceed to gate seventeen where the flight is now boarding.

Jools (*to himself*) Oh — bother! (*He looks at his watch again and then sighs. He gets his tickets and passport out of his pocket and turns to the check-in desk*)

Just as Jools turns, the Check-in Man (played by the same actor who played Costos) pops up cheerily behind the check-in desk, making Jools jump

Oh!

Check-in Man (*London suburban accent; cheerily*) Good-afternoon, sir.

Jools (*handing over his ticket and passport*) Oh — yes — er — Cork.

Check-in Man Cork, sir.

Jools Yes — er — two twenty.

Check-in Man (*looking at the documents*) Two twenty. Cutting it a bit fine, aren't we, sir?

Jools Er ... Yes — sorry. I was waiting for someone.

Check-in Man Oh. Not shown, eh, sir?

Jools Not yet. No.

Check-in Man She'll have to be quick. The flight's started boarding.

Jools She?

Check-in Man The person you're waiting for?

Jools Oh — yes — she.

Check-in Man Is that all your luggage, sir?

Jools Um — yes. (*He puts his case on the scales*)

Check-in Man Did you pack the case yourself, sir?

Jools Er — yes.

Check-in Man Any electronic equipment in your luggage, sir?

Jools Er — no.

Check-in Man (*putting a label on the case and taking it behind the desk*)
That's all hunky dory, then. (*He sorts out a boarding card and hands it to Jools with the other documents*) Here we are, sir. It's gate seventeen.

Jools Good. Er ... If my friend does arrive in time, could I possibly leave her ticket with you? *I've* got it, you see.

Check-in Man You can, sir, but if she's not here in the next two minutes she'll've missed it.

Jools (*producing a second ticket and handing to to the man*) Good. Her name's Helen. Helen Richards.

Check-in Man (*taking the ticket*) Helen Richards. Right you are, sir.

Helen rushes on, breathless, with an overnight bag in her hand

Helen Jools!
Jools (*spinning round*) Helen!
Check-in Man Helen!

Jools and Helen turn to the Check-in Man. Helen looks at him curiously

Jools (*to Helen*) Give the man your passport. You've nearly missed it.

Helen holds out her passport to the Check-in Man, still looking at him curiously

Helen Er ...
Check-in Man (*taking the passport; cheerfully and in a business-like manner*) Thank you, Helen ... I mean, madam.
Helen Er — —
Jools (*interrupting*) I thought you weren't coming.
Helen (*to Jools*) I thought I wasn't. (*A slight pause*) Here I am.
Check-in Man Is that all your luggage, madam?
Helen Er ... Yes.
Check-in Man Put your bag on the scales, please, madam.
Helen (*doing so; to Jools*) Is this all right? I mean — hallo — is this all right? You haven't changed your mind?
Check-in Man Did you pack the case yourself, madam?
Helen Yes.
Check-in Man Any electronic equipment in your luggage, madam?
Helen No.

A sudden, muffled but distinct electronic crying rings out from the bag

That is, except for the irritating baby in the bottom of my bathroom bag.

Check-in Man Baby, madam? (*He stares at Helen, puzzled*)
Jools (*concerned*) Have you been looking after her?
Helen I've tried my best, but when she started up at three o'clock this morning, I nearly binned her.
Jools Don't bin her. I want to see how well she lasts.

Jools and Helen become aware of the puzzled stare of the Check-in Man

(*To the Man*) It's nothing. Honestly. It's just a toy.
Check-in Man A toy. I see, sir.
Jools It won't show up on anything. Or interfere. It's nothing. It'll stop in a minute.

The crying stops

There. I told you.
Check-in Man (*dubiously*) You did, sir.
Tannoy This is the last call for passengers for Aer Lingus flight EI oh-seven-one-five to Cork. Will passengers for Aer Lingus flight EI oh-seven-one-five to Cork please proceed to gate seventeen where the flight is about to depart.
Check-in Man (*sorting out a boarding card and handing it to Helen with the other documents*) You'd better hurry. Here's your boarding card, madam.
Helen (*taking the documents*) Thank you. (*To Jools*) I mean, is this all right?
Jools It's wonderful.
Helen But — —
Check-in Man (*to Helen urgently*) It's wonderful! Now get a move on!
Jools (*holding out his hand to indicate the way to Helen*) Here.

Helen unthinkingly takes Jool's hand. They find themselves holding hands again. This time they don't let go straight away

Helen Oh.

They share a moment

Check-in Man (*urgently*) Get a move on! Gate number seventeen!
Helen (*letting go of Jools' hand*) Yes.
Jools (*hurrying Helen off*) Come on.
Helen (*over her shoulder, to the Man*) I'm sure I know you from somewhere.
Check-in Man (*despairingly*) Hurry up, Helen!

Helen and Jools hurry off

"Runaway" by the Corrs plays

   The Check-in Man dismantles the check-in desk and exits with the cases

The Lights cross-fade to the next scene

SCENE 4

The aeroplane

Helen and Jools enter and set up the aeroplane (See p.58) and sit side by side

The music fades to a lower level

Jools Oh — by the way — here you are. (*He holds out some money to Helen*)
Helen What's this?
Jools For my salad.
Helen Oh — don't be silly.
Jools I'm not. Go on. Take it. I insist.
Helen (*reluctantly taking it*) Oh — go on then.

There is a slight pause

Jools How was the hotel?
Helen Lonely.

   *The Stewardess (played by the same actor who played the Check-in Man)
   trundles down the aisle with a trolley*

Stewardess (*to Helen*) Would you like a drink, madam?

Helen stares very hard at the Stewardess

The music fades up to its full level again

   The Stewardess trundles her trolley further down the plane and exits

   Helen and Jools dismantle the aeroplane and exit

The Lights cross-fade to the next scene

SCENE 5

A Cork hotel

*The Irish Hotel Receptionist (played by the same actor who played the
Stewardess) enters and sets up the hotel lounge. (See p.58) Then he settles
himself behind the reception desk*

Helen and Jools enter with their cases and go up to the reception desk

The music cross-fades into bland hotel foyer Muzak

Helen stares at the Irish Receptionist during the following

Irish Receptionist (*very broad Southern Irish accent*) Welcome to the
Starkright Hotel, Cork, sir and madam, a member of White House plc. How
may I help you?

Jools Er ... (*He looks at Helen, who is still staring, and back again at the Irish
Receptionist*) I've got a reservation.

Irish Receptionist A reservation, is it, sir? T'at's fine.

Jools That is ... *I've* got a reservation — but Helen Richards here hasn't.

Irish Receptionist And what might t'e name be, sir?

Jools I've just said — Helen Richards.

Irish Receptionist Ah ... No ... sir. I'm afraid we've been talking at cross
purposes t'ere. It's your own name t'at I'm after at t'e moment.

Jools Oh — yes — er — sorry — of course. Er ... It's Baker. Julian Baker.

Irish Receptionist Well, t'ere we are t'en. I have you here. And t'e young
lady's wanting to stay for two nights as well, is she?

Jools (*with a look at Helen, who is still staring*) Er ... Yes. Yes, that's right.

Irish Receptionist T'at's grand. Now t'en, is it a double room you're after
here?

Jools Oh! Er ... (*He looks at Helen*) Helen ... Helen!

Helen (*coming out of her stare*) Yes? What?

Jools The room — er — the *room*. Single? Double?

Helen (*trying to work out the implications*) Oh ... Double ... Er?

There is a slight pause

Jools (*helpfully*) Single?

Helen (*playing safe*) Yes. Single.

Jools Single. (*To the Irish Receptionist*) Single.

Irish Receptionist Single. T'at's fine, sir. Madam. Now, as luck would have
it, t'ere's a single room free just next to t'e one I've already got down here
for you, sir.

Jools Oh — good.

Irish Receptionist So if you'd just like to sign at t'e bottom t'ere.

Jools OK. (*He signs the register*)

Irish Receptionist Madam?

Helen Thank you. (*She signs*)

Irish Receptionist (*handing over room keys*) Here we are, t'en. Number one-one-eight and one-one-nine, right up t'ere on t'e first floor. Would you like anyone to be helping you wit' your luggage at all?

Jools (*feeling his pockets for change for a tip*) Er ... no. No thanks. We'll be OK. (*With a look at Helen*) I think. (*To Helen*) Are you all right?

Helen What?

Jools Are you all right?

Helen Yes. I'm fine. (*Under her breath*) Haven't you noticed?

Jools (*under his breath*) What?

Helen Well!

Jools What?

Helen Everyone we meet. They all look the same.

Jools Do they?

Helen Yes. (*Indicating the Irish Receptionist*) Look.

Jools looks at the Irish Receptionist

Jools No. I don't think so. Must be a trick of the light or something. (*To the Irish Receptionist, with a smile*) Sorry.

Irish Receptionist T'at's all right, sir.

Helen has another look at the Irish Receptionist

Helen There must be something very funny about the light at the moment then.

Irish Receptionist I've not done anything wrong, I hope.

Jools Oh no. No.

Helen No. I was just wondering ... (*She dries up*)

Irish Receptionist Wondering what, madam?

Helen Well — you're not a member of a very large family, are you?

Irish Receptionist Ah. No. T'ere I'm afraid I can't help you, madam.

Helen Oh?

Irish Receptionist No. You see, I'm t'e only one. Me poor mother, God rest her soul ... Well, she wasn't as strong as she might've been — and I was a bit of a struggle coming, if you know what I mean — and me father — well, he was a good man — and not so devoted a Cat'lic t'at he minded using a bit o' rubber every now and t'en. So here you see me — t'e only one.

Helen Ah.

Irish Receptionist What was running t'rough your mind t'en, madam? Enquiring about t'e size of me family?

Helen Well, it's just that … Oh, it sounds so silly, but — everyone I meet at the moment seems to me to be practically the same person.

Irish Receptionist Now t'at is strange, madam.

Helen I think it is.

Irish Receptionist And I'm one of t'ese people, am I, madam?

Helen Yes … yes, you are.

Irish Receptionist I t'ink I know what it is.

Helen You do?

Irish Receptionist I t'ink I do.

There is a slight pause

Helen Go on then.

Irish Receptionist Well, you know how, in a play sometimes, you get one actor playing lots o' parts, and t'ere he is trying to make t'em all look different?

Helen Yes?

Irish Receptionist Well, I'm t'e opposite of t'at. I'm one of lots of different people who just happen by chance to look t'e same.

There is a slight pause

Helen Ah.

Irish Receptionist T'ere you are t'en, madam. T'at's cleared t'at one up for you.

Helen (*dubiously*) Yes. Thank you.

Irish Receptionist T'ink not'ing of it. Now t'en, don't t'e two of you be forgetting to enjoy our beautiful scenery while you're staying wit' us here. I want to see you bot' up on t'ose cliffs t'ere, looking out to sea, wit' t'e fields behind yer. Won't t'at be nice now?

There is a slight pause

Jools Lovely.

There is a slight pause

The sudden, muffled electronic crying starts up. The Irish Receptionist looks puzzled

Helen (*to the Irish Receptionist*) Don't ask.

The crying dissolves into the noise of crashing waves

   The Irish Receptionist exits

The Lights cross-fade to the next scene

SCENE 6

The cliffs. Afternoon

Helen and Jools arrange the cliff setting (See p. 58)

Helen He was right. It's beautiful. (*Pause*) Couldn't you stay here forever?
Jools Yes. (*Pause*) And no.
Helen No?
Jools I have to go to Los Angeles tomorrow.
Jools Oh. Yes. (*Pause*) How did it go this morning?
Jools Oh — good. Quite a lot of interest.
Helen What is it? This new toy.
Jools It's a water pistol.
Helen That's not very new, is it?
Jools It's computerized. Every now and then — after a random number of
   forward squirts — it fires one off in an unexpected direction.
Helen Oh.
Jools It adds an element of surprise. Kids like that.
Helen Yes.
Jools And it makes it very expensive. Kids like that too. (*Pause*) Are you glad
   you came?

Helen thinks

Helen Yes. Yes, I am. (*Pause*) Are you? ... Glad I came?
Jools Yes. Of course.
Helen It's good — just to be somewhere different. Clear my head.
Jools I haven't got in the way.
Helen (*with a smile*) No. No, of course you haven't. (*Pause. Looking into
   Jools' eyes*) Dinner last night was lovely. (*Pause*) I phoned my friend
   Rachel this morning.
Jools Oh?
Helen She's working in the Gulf for six months. I can stay in her flat. Till
   she comes back.

Jools Ah.
Helen It'll give me a bit of time.
Jools Yes.
Helen To sort something permanent out.
Jools Of course. (*Pause*) You could always come to LA with me.
Helen Jools!
Jools If you wanted to. Be somewhere else different. (*Slight pause*) Clear
   your head a bit more. (*He looks into her eyes. Slight pause*) All paid for.
Helen (*looking into his eyes*) I've got a horrible feeling my head's cleared
   as much as it's going to.

Pause

Jools Have you?

Pause

Helen Yes.

They kiss, then break and smile at each other

Helen LA it is, then.

"Rockin' All Over the World" by Status Quo crashes in

Helen and Jools move back to their cases

The Lights cross-fade to the next scene

Scene 7

A Los Angeles hotel

*The American Hotel Receptionist (played by the same actor who played the
Irish Receptionist), enters behind the reception desk*

The music cross-fades into the same bland hotel foyer Muzak

American Receptionist (*American accent*) Welcome to the Starkright
   Hotel, Los Angeles, sir and madam, a member of White House plc. How
   may I help you?

*Jools looks enquiringly at Helen. She gives a resigned, amused, affirmative
acknowledgement back. Jools turns back to the American Receptionist*

Jools Yes. I've got a reservation.

American Receptionist Very good, sir. What name, please?

Jools Baker. Julian Baker. Helen Richards here wants to stay as well, but she hasn't got a reservation.

American Receptionist Certainly, sir. Would madam like a single room or would sir like to exchange his for a double?

Jools (*to Helen; hopefully*) Single? Double?

Helen (*to Jools; with a smile*) Double.

Jools (*to Helen*) Double. (*To the American Receptionist*) Double.

American Receptionist Double. Very good, sir. If you'd both care to sign right here.

Jools and Helen both sign the register

(*Giving them the key*) Room five-eight-six. The elevator's right over there. Enjoy your stay.

Jools and Helen smile at each other and move to the opposite side of the stage. They arrange the bedroom setting and get into bed (See P.58)

The Lights cross-fade to the next scene

SCENE 8

The Los Angeles hotel room. Morning

Helen and Jools are sitting up in bed together. The Muzak fades out

Jools I have to get up.

Helen Must you?

Jools I have a toy pistol to promote.

Helen (*with a twinkle*) Oh, really!

Jools smiles. They kiss

Pause

Jools Are you happy?

Helen Very. (*Pause*) Are you?

Jools Very.

Pause

Helen (*with a twinkle*) I've never been to Japan.

Jools laughs and tickles Helen

"Rockin' All Over the World" crashes in

Helen and Jools return to the reception desk

The Lights cross-fade to the next scene

Scene 9

A Tokyo hotel

The Japanese Hotel Receptionist, looking very cod Japanese, (played by the same actor who played the American Receptionist) enters behind the reception desk

The music cross-fades into the same bland hotel foyer Muzak

The Japanese Receptionist bows ceremoniously to Helen and Jools, who awkwardly bow back

Japanese Receptionist (*Wolverhampton accent*) Welcome to the Starkright Hotel, Tokyo, sir and madam, a member of White House plc. How may I help you?

Jools and Helen stare at the Japanese Receptionist

Jools Er — yes — Julian Baker — er …
Japanese Receptionist (*interrupting*) Oh! You're English, aren't you?
Jools Er — yes.
Japanese Receptionist Now I know what you're thinking. I got meself a transfer from Wolverhampton, didn't I? Fancied meself a bit of a change, like.
Jools Oh … Good.
Japanese Receptionist Have you got a reservation then?
Jools Er — yes. I've got a single room reserved. But I'd like to exchange it for — (*he turns to Helen*) a double?
Helen (*promptly*) A double.
Jools (*back to the Japanese Receptionist; confidently*) A double. If that's possible, please? With Helen Richards here.
Japanese Receptionist A double room. Right you are, sir. Will you sign here, please?

Helen and Jools move to sign the register. The muffled, electronic crying starts up. Helen kicks the case. It stops abruptly

Jools and Helen smile at the Japanese Receptionist and move to the bedroom

The Lights cross-fade to the next scene

SCENE 10

A Tokyo hotel room. Morning

Helen and Jools are sitting up in bed together

The Muzak fades out

Jools I don't know about everybody we meet looking the same. All these hotel rooms are the same.

Pause

Helen I expect the one in Moscow will be, as well.
Jools Cheeky.

"Rockin' All Over the World" crashes in

Helen and Jools return to the reception desk

The Lights cross-fade to the next scene

SCENE 11

A Moscow hotel

The Russian Hotel Receptionist (played by the same actor who played the Japanese Receptionist) enters behind the reception desk

The music cross-fades into the same bland hotel foyer Muzak

Russian Receptionist (*Russian accent*) Welcome to the Starkright Hotel, Moscow, sir and madam, a member of White House plc. How may I help you?
Jools Double room, please. I've got a single room booked but I'd like to exchange it.

Helen and Jools move to the bedroom

The Lights cross-fade to the next scene

SCENE 12

A Moscow hotel room. Evening

Helen and Jools are sitting up in bed together. The Muzak fades out

Helen When do we go home?
Jools When we like.

Pause

Helen Can we stay on here a bit?
Jools If you like. (*Pause*) Just for a bit.
Helen It's romantic here.
Jools In Moscow?
Helen Don't laugh at me. It's like we're having a sort of honeymoon.
Jools (*with a kindly laugh*) I love you.
Helen Only say that if you mean it.

Pause

Jools I love you … Come here.

Jools rolls Helen over

"Say It Again" by Precious starts to play

Helen and Jools set up the bridge (See p. 59)

The Lights cross-fade to the next scene

SCENE 13

A bridge over the Moskva. Moscow. Frosty morning

Jools and Helen are leaning on the bridge, looking down at the water

The music fades

Pause

Helen I love *you*.

Jools smiles

Jools You're right. It is romantic.

Pause

Helen What are we going to do?

Pause

Jools Do?
Helen When we get back. (*Pause*) We'll be back tomorrow, what shall we do?

Pause

Jools I'll call you.
Helen (*taken aback*) Call me?

Pause

Jools Yes.

Pause

Helen That's not what I meant.
Jools I can't see you round to Rachel's, I'm afraid. Sorry. Jane's meeting me at the airport.
Helen Jane?
Jools It's the kids' birthday. I promised I'd be there. For their party.

Pause

Helen She's meeting you at the airport.
Jools Yes.
Helen How does she know you'll be there? You were supposed to be home three days ago.
Jools I called her. Last night. (*Pause*) We'd give you a lift — but ... Maybe not a good idea. For Jane.

Helen No.

Pause

The electronic crying suddenly starts up. Helen grabs the toy out of her pocket and hurls it into the river

Jools (*looking after the toy*) It needs some modifications anyway. (*Pause*) I *want* to. It's my kids' party. (*Pause*) Shall I see you back at the hotel?

Pause

Jools exits

A ship's hooter sounds

Black-out

Rachel's flat. (See p. 59) Evening

There are a CD remote, a telephone, a bottle of gin and a glass in the room. Helen's bag is by the door

"End of the Line" by the Honeyz plays

As the scene begins, the volume of the music decreases

Helen is sitting alone. She seems sad. She looks at the phone, then looks away again. She goes to lift the receiver, but decides against it, going instead to pour herself a glass of gin, which she sits and drinks

The doorbell rings

Helen reacts excitedly. She turns down the volume of the music a bit more with the remote and opens the front door

A young man — a Pizza Delivery Man —stands in the doorway, holding a pizza box. He is played by the same actor as the Russian Receptionist

Helen doesn't recognize the young man

Helen (*disappointed*) Oh.
Pizza Delivery Man (*Scottish*) Here's your pizza.
Helen What?
Pizza Delivery Man Your pizza. You ordered a pizza.
Helen Oh! Yes. Did I? I'd forgotten all about it.
Pizza Delivery Man You only ordered it thirty-five minutes ago.
Helen Did I?
Pizza Delivery Man It's bang on time.
Helen Yes.
Pizza Delivery Man No refund for late delivery.
Helen No.

Pizza Delivery Man (*handing over the pizza*) Double pepperoni. You'll like it.
Helen I'm sure. Er … How much is it?

Helen starts to search for her purse in the bag beside the door

Pizza Delivery Man Six pounds fifty. The delivery's two pounds extra, as it's under a tenner.
Helen OK.
Pizza Delivery Man I'm sorry.
Helen No. That's fine. (*Handing the Pizza Delivery Man a ten pound note*) There you are. Keep the change.
Pizza Delivery Man Are you sure?
Helen Yes, of course. Thank you.
Pizza Delivery Man Thanks.

Helen goes to shut the door

(*As an afterthought*) Are you all right?
Helen Yes. Why?
Pizza Delivery Man Only you look terrible.
Helen Thanks. I feel terrible, but I'm fine.
Pizza Delivery Man What's the matter?
Helen Oh, it's nothing.
Pizza Delivery Man It doesna' look like nothing.
Helen Oh … I'm missing a man, that's all.
Pizza Delivery Man Oh. You're right. It's nothing. You'll soon get over it.
Helen I'm sure I will.
Pizza Delivery Man Or maybe's he'll phone. You never know.
Helen He may.
Pizza Delivery Man Goodbye, then … Enjoy your pizza.
Helen I will. Goodbye. (*She closes the door. To herself*) "He took me all over the world, then dumped me." (*She gives a little cynical laugh*) It'll make an article for "Take a Break" if nothing else! (*She turns the volume of the music up again, sits, opens the pizza box and starts to eat, very dejectedly*)

The phone rings

Helen excitedly throws the pizza aside, turns the volume down again and answers the phone

Hallo? (*Warmly*) Oh, hallo. … No, no, no, that's all right. … Yes. I've been busy too. … Yes. I'd like that. Very much. … Shall I meet you there? …

Half an hour, right. ... Er, Jools. ... No, it's nothing. ... Sorry. ... I love you.

Helen puts the phone down, turns "End of the Line" off on the CD with the remote and turns on "Dancing in the Moonlight" by Toploader very loud

Jools enters with a pint of bitter and a cocktail

Together, having fun to the music, Jools and Helen dismantle Rachel's flat and set up the club (See p. 59)

The Lights cross-fade to the next scene

SCENE 2

Nightclub

Suddenly Helen and Jools stand about gloomily and slightly aimlessly with their drinks. The music continues to play, at a slightly lower volume

Pause

Jools (*shouting above the music*) This is horrible.
Helen (*not hearing; shouting above the music*) What?
Jools (*louder*) This is horrible.
Helen I thought you wanted to come.
Jools Me?
Helen Yes.
Jools I only came because of you.
Helen What?
Jools I only came because of you.
Helen Me?
Jools Yes.
Helen I hate clubbing.
Jools Do you?
Helen I hate it.
Jools So do I.
Helen *You* do?
Jools I've always hated it. Ever since I was a teenager. Every five years or so I think to myself, "No, I'm wrong. I must enjoy it really." So I go along, have an argument at the door because I'm wearing the wrong trousers, spend too much on drinks and end up deaf for the next two days, thus proving I was absolutely right in the first place. I hate clubbing. Well, here I am again — and the five years aren't even up yet.
Helen Then what are we doing here?
Jools I thought you wanted to come.

Helen I'd've gone anywhere rather than this.

Jools Would you?

Helen I'd've even gone back to that tiny little pub theatre we went to last week.

Jools What? On those hard seats?

Helen Yes.

Jools Even to see that three-and-a-half-hour one-man version of *Pride and Prejudice*?

Helen Even to see that.

The DJ announces the next track and the music changes to "Eternal Flame" by Atomic Kitten which plays a little quieter than the last music

Jools We could've had a night in.

Helen That would've been nice.

Jools Especially as we've been out every night this week.

Helen Yes.

Jools Still, we may as well finish these drinks now. We've paid for them.

Helen OK.

There is a slight pause

Jools The kids are really looking forward to tomorrow.

Helen So am I. I can't wait to meet them.

Jools Mind you, knowing them, it's probably the going to the zoo bit they're excited about, not the bit about meeting you.

Helen I'm sure.

Jools Sorry about that.

Helen Don't worry. I've got a younger sister. I know what kids are like. (*Pause*) What time are we picking them up?

Jools Ten o'clock.

Helen Right.

Jools I'll just nip along and collect them while you wait at the tube station.

Helen What?

Jools I'll nip along and collect them.

Helen Why can't I nip along with you?

Jools (*taken aback*) Oh … Well — I hadn't thought of that.

Helen I might as well. It'll be a good opportunity to say "Hallo".

Jools "Hallo"?

Helen Yes. To Jane.

Jools Oh … I don't know.

Helen Just on the doorstep. Nothing more.

Jools Don't you think it'll be a bit awkward?

Helen Oh. Will it?

Jools For you and Jane.

Helen Well, we've got to meet sometime.

Jools I know.

Helen She's quite happy about you and me, isn't she?

Jools Oh … yes.

Helen I mean, you two splitting up was her idea, wasn't it?

Jools Yes.

Helen In the first place.

Jools That's right.

Helen And you're happy about it too, aren't you?

Jools Of course I am.

Helen Oh, please, tell me you are, because I think I'm starting to love you an awful lot.

Jools I'm happy about it. I adore you.

Helen Then we may as well just say "Hallo".

Jools (*suddenly seeing someone*) Oh no!

Helen What's the matter?

Jools Look who's there.

Helen (*looking*) Where?

Jools (*pointing without trying to be too obvious*) Over there. In the green shirt.

Helen Oh, my God. It's Pete!

Jools Do you want to go?

Helen Who's he with?

Jools I don't know.

Helen She's very young.

Jools I don't know her.

Helen Well. I won't worry about *him* any more, then.

Jools Oh. Were you?

Helen What?

Jools Worrying about him?

Helen Well — a little. Yes, of course I was.

Jools (*looking at Pete*) It's probably just on the rebound.

Helen Do you think so?

Jools Oh yes.

Helen Have you spoken to him?

Jools No. Have you?

Helen No. I must. I owe him some money for bills.

Jools It looks like bills are the last thing on his mind at the moment.

Helen Yes. (*Slight pause*) I'm pleased. (*Putting her arms round Jools*) What about us, then?

Jools What about us?

Helen Are we just on the rebound?
Jools (*responding*) Oh, definitely!

The DJ announces the next track and the music changes to "Reach for the Stars" by S Club 7

Helen Oh, I love this. Come on! Let's give in and go and bounce around on the dance floor a bit.
Jools (*reluctantly*) Oh, no, Helen …
Helen Come on. Just for this once.
Jools No. You'll see what a prat I am dancing and fall out of love with me. It's not worth the risk.
Helen I'm prepared to take it.
Jools But — (*clutching at straws*) Pete'll see us together.
Helen I hope he does. It's about time he knew the horrible truth. (*She pulls him towards the dance floor*)
Jools (*a wail of despair*) Oh …

The volume of the music increases

Helen drags Jools on to the dance floor. Helen dances well. Jools dances like a man. They're both having a good time

An Ageing Playboy (played by the same actor who played the Pizza Delivery Man) enters and joins them on the dance floor and dances eccentrically, but very well

Helen and Jools exit dancing

Still dancing, the Ageing Playboy sets up the zoo (see p. 41) — including a bench — and exits

The music fades

The Lights cross-fade to the next scene

SCENE 3

The zoo

Assorted animal noises and noises of children playing in an adventure playground

Helen enters carrying two children's backpacks. Jools enters backwards carrying an adult backpack, calling out to one side of the auditorium as if to two children who are getting further away as he shouts

Jools Just twenty minutes! Then it's the penguins' feeding time. We're just over here if you want us. Emmy! Be careful. Mind you don't kick Stephen in the face! (*To himself*) Oh God!

Helen (*sitting on a bench*) Will they be OK?

Jools (*backing over to sit next to Helen, keeping his eyes on the children*) Oh, yes. Trust them to be more interested in an adventure playground than all the animals.

Helen (*getting some sandwiches out of the adult bag*) Emmy loved the chimpanzees.

Jools Only because she is one herself!

Helen She's lovely. They both are.

Jools Thank you.

Helen (*giving Jools a sandwich*) Stephen was brilliant making up that story about the gorilla.

Jools Yes. (*For the sandwich*) Thanks.

Helen (*taking a sandwich herself*) What did he call the gorilla?

Jools Toffee.

Helen That's right.

Jools Everyone's called Toffee at the moment. His best friend's just got a cat called Toffee.

Helen Oh, I see.

Jools He's always making up stories. He takes after his mum.

Helen Does he?

Jools It's Emmy that takes after me. She loves taking things apart. Trying to see how they work. When she was three — nearly four — she took the bag out of the vacuum cleaner. It wasn't plugged in, thank God. I was working. There was dust everywhere. Jane was furious. Oh! (*He goes to run to the playground but sits again*) That's one thing she doesn't get from either of us. The daredevil bit. We're neither of us very adventurous.

Helen (*eating her sandwich*) She's very beautiful.

Jools Well, I think so, of course.

Helen Who?

Jools Emmy. She was beautiful even when she was just born.

Helen No. I meant Jane.

Jools Oh. Do you think so?

Helen Don't you?

Jools I suppose so.

Helen She's gorgeous. (*A slight pause*) Jools — why are you leaving her?

Jools Because I don't love her any more.

Helen But she's gorgeous.

Jools I don't think she's anything like as beautiful as you.

Helen Oh, don't be silly.

Jools I mean it.

The Zoo-keeper (played by the same actor who played the Ageing Playboy)
enters with a bucket as if to cross the stage.

Jools (*to the Zoo-keeper*) Oh, excuse me. What time do the penguins feed?
Zoo-keeper (*without turning to Jools and Helen, on the move, in a pseudo-
posh sergeant major accent*) Penguins at two-thirty. Seals just before then
at two-fifteen. I'm on my way for the fish now.

The Zoo-keeper exits

Jools Oh. I was wrong. (*Shouting to the children*) Emmy! Stephen! Do you
want to go and see the seals have their dinner? ... The seals! ... No? All
right then. Have another twenty minutes here, but then we're definitely
going to see the penguins. Stephen! Don't throw the sand! You're five
years old now! Stephen!

There is a slight pause

Helen This is very nice.
Jools (*smiling*) What?
Helen You and me. Sitting here like this. With the children.
Jools Do you like it?
Helen Yes. Do you mind?
Jools Mind? Why should I mind?
Helen Well ... I'm sort of taking advantage of your ready-made family.
Jools You're not taking advantage of anything. This is just how it is.
Helen Yes?
Jools And you're right.
Helen What?
Jools It is very nice.

Pause. They eat and watch the children

Helen Do you think they like me?
Jools Oh, yes.
Helen I think they do.
Jools You can see they do. Stephen held your hand. That's a very great
compliment.

Pause

Listen.
Helen What?

Jools I've been doing some serious thinking.
Helen (*teasingly*) Oh dear.
Jools Yes.
Helen And what's the result? An exploding *teddy bear*?
Jools No! Not about work! About us.
Helen Oh. What about us?
Jools Well ... You and me — we get on OK, don't we?
Helen (*jokingly appalled*) "OK"?
Jools (*suddenly worried*) Well, don't we?
Helen Jools, we get on brilliantly.
Jools (*relieved*) Ah. Yes. That's what I thought. And not only that, I love you very much.
Helen I know. You've told me.
Jools I have. Quite a few times.
Helen Quite a few.
Jools The thing is — do *you* love *me*?
Helen You know I do. I've told you *that* quite a few times as well.
Jools Yes.
Helen You know I have.
Jools Yes, I do.
Helen Lots of times.
Jools Yes.
Helen Oodles of times.
Jools That's right.
Helen Oodles and scroodles of times.
Jools Yes. OK. I just wanted to make sure.

There is a slight pause

Helen So?
Jools So ... I was just thinking ...
Helen Yes?
Jools Well — since we seem to be spending practically all our time together ...
Helen We are.
Jools When we're not working, of course.
Helen Of course.
Jools Well — don't you think it's time we actually moved in together?
Helen (*slightly embarrassedly*) Oh.
Jools Don't you think so.
Helen Move in together?
Jools Yes.
Helen Oh.

Jools I mean, to be honest, we're practically living together already, aren't we?

Helen Are we?

Jools Well, every night we're either at your flat — —

Helen Rachel's flat.

Jools Yes. Rachel's flat ... Or we're at mine.

Helen It's true.

Jools So. (*Pause*) What do you think?

Pause

Helen Jools, I love you so much.

Jools Yes. We've just cleared that one up.

Helen I've been hoping and hoping we'd actually end up living together sometime — in the same flat — or house — or tent ... I don't really care ...

Jools Well, I thought my flat, probably.

Helen Yes, if you like.

Jools (*moving to hug Helen*) Oh, Helen ...

Helen (*not responding*) But not yet.

Jools What?

Helen I don't want to move in with you yet.

Jools But I thought you just said — —

Helen Look — it's probably silly of me — or maybe I'm just hopelessly old-fashioned or something — but I don't think I actually want to move in with you until you're divorced from Jane.

Jools What?

Helen Or at least until you've started the whole thing going.

The Zoo-keeper enters the way he last exited with a bucket full of fish

Zoo-keeper (*without turning to Jools and Helen, on the move*) Last call for the seals. I've got me fish.

Helen (*to the Zoo-keeper*) We're giving the seals a miss.

Zoo-keeper Penguins at two-thirty.

The Zoo-keeper exits

Jools Helen ...

Helen You haven't actually done anything about it yet, have you?

Jools Well ...

Helen Either of you?

Jools Well — no ... But ...

Helen Well, when are you going to? It's nearly a year and a half now since you moved out.

Jools Look, it's not as simple as that, is it? We've got to think of the kids.

Helen I thought you said it was better for the kids.

Jools What?

Helen You said you and Jane were getting on better since you moved out.

Jools Well ... Yes, we are — but ...

Helen But what?

Jools Well ... Mummy and Daddy getting divorced — that's a whole new ball game, isn't it?

Helen Oh, no. I'm sorry. They're only five. You're not going to tell me they understand the meaning of the word "divorce" at their age. What're you going to do? Wait until they're twelve or thirteen and ask them if they mind?

Jools (*intensely*) You'd be amazed at how much they understand. Suddenly, for no reason, Daddy doesn't come to read them a story in bed every night. And he's not there in bed with Mummy when they wake up in the morning. For some reason, he comes knocking at the front door — after they've got dressed. Of course they understand.

Pause

Helen Hey you ... I'm sorry. I didn't mean this to get so heavy.

Jools Neither did I. *I'm* sorry. (*Suddenly looking to the children and panicking*) Oh God! Where is she? (*Seeing her*) Oh. (*Shouting to the children*) Emmy! For goodness' sake, be careful!

Pause

Helen Look — you're living apart already. Please. Just get divorced. It can't make any difference.

Jools Exactly! It can't make any difference. So move in with me.

Helen (*urgently again*) It would just make me feel better, all right? It would stop it hurting so much ...

Jools Stop what hurting?

Helen When you see her all the time.

Jools See her? See who?

Helen Jane.

Jools Jane?

Helen Who do you think I'm talking about?

Jools I don't see her all the time.

Helen Yes, you do.

Jools Only when it's to do with the kids.

Helen I know. But that's three or four times a week.
Jools Not always.
Helen Sometimes more. Just think of me a bit.
Jools I do. All the time.

The Zoo-keeper enters from the side he just exited from, with his bucket empty

Zoo-keeper (*without turning to Jools and Helen, on the move*) My life is ruled by the feeding habits of salt-water animals.

The Zoo-keeper exits

Helen I find it really hard to cope, all right?
Jools What?
Helen You going round to that house a lot — where the two of you used to live together.
Jools Oh, don't be silly.
Helen It's not silly!
Jools I *have* to go round there, don't I?
Helen Do you?
Jools Of course I do! I can't expect Jane to drop the kids up to Finsbury Park every time I want to see them.
Helen It's not the kids I'm worried about.
Jools (*taken aback*) Um ... Are you saying you think there's still something going on between us?
Helen I don't know. Is there?
Jools After all I've said to you? After I've asked you to move in with me?
Helen There could be.
Jools Helen ... (*Demanding her attention*) Helen! ... I haven't slept with Jane for over two years now. We've got absolutely nothing in common with each other. Apart from the kids.
Helen Well, you seem bloody reluctant to get divorced.
Jools But that's different.
Helen Why?
Jools It's different!
Helen Why?
Jools (*exasperatedly*) It's just different!!!
Helen How do I know you're not going to bed with her whenever you're round there?
Jools Oh, don't be ridiculous!
Helen But how do I *know?*
Jools Because I've told you.

Helen Big deal!

Jools What?

Helen She hasn't got anyone else, has she? She must be itching to sleep with you again, just to spite me!

Jools Oh for God's sake! Jane's not like that.

Helen You're a man, aren't you?

Jools What's that supposed to mean?

Helen Well — why not? Just for old times' sake.

Jools What sort of person do you think I am?

Helen I don't know. You could be just a two-timing bastard.

Jools What?

Helen I've known enough of them!

Jools I'm not!

Helen You could be.

Jools (*finally*) I'm *not!*

Jools turns away from Helen

There is a slight pause

Helen (*desperately*) Please. Don't go round there.

Jools turns back to Helen

Jools Oh, all right! All right! Helen, I love you. I love you so much, but — sorry! Go away!

Helen What?

Jools Just — go away! I can't cope with this.

Helen Jools ...

Jools I can't ... I *won't* give up my kids.

Helen (*taken aback*) I'm not asking you to.

Jools I won't give them up!

Helen I'm not asking you to.

Jools Oh — go away. (*Slight pause*) Go away!

Pause. They stare at each other

Are you deaf as well as stupid?

There is a slight pause

Helen All right. (*Slight pause*) What'll you tell the kids?

Jools I'll tell them you're sick. I'll tell them you're dead. I don't care. Just go away!

Helen exits

Jools sits on the bench and cries

The Zoo-keeper enters from the side he has just exited from with his bucket full of fish

Zoo-keeper (*without turning to Jools, on the move*) Penguins it is, then.
Jools (*to himself; in anguish*) Oh no!
Zoo-keeper (*without turning to Jools, on the move*) Well. It's not compulsory.
Jools (*a shout of frustration*) Agh!
Zoo-keeper (*without turning to Jools, on the move*) They'll still be here tomorrow if you don't fancy it today.
Jools Oh — bugger the penguins!
Zoo-keeper (*stopping in his tracks and looking at Jools*) I beg your pardon?
Jools (*to the Zoo-keeper*) I'm sorry.
Zoo-keeper What've my penguins ever done to you?
Jools No. It's not the penguins.
Keeper They're good animals, penguins.
Jools I'm sure.
Zoo-keeper They trust you. Mind you, you have to earn it.
Jools Oh yes?
Zoo-keeper It's no use thinking they'll stick by you willy-nilly.
Jools Is this some sort of grotesque metaphor?
Zoo-keeper What?
Jools Metaphor.
Zoo-keeper That's enough language from you. I'll not hear a word said against my penguins.
Jools I'm sorry. I take it all back.
Zoo-keeper Glad to hear it. (*Looking at a clock in distance*) Two thirty-one. I'm a bit behind time today. Come now if you're coming. They don't like to be kept waiting.

The Zoo-keeper exits

Jools sits quietly for a few moments, watching the children. His eyes fill with tears. With an effort, he pulls himself together

Jools (*shouting*) Emmy! Stephen! Penguins! (*He waits impatiently for a few moments, then shouts irritably*) Come on!

"Sometimes" by Britney Spears plays

Jools takes two imaginary children by the hand and slowly walks off with them

The Lights cross-fade to the next scene

SCENE 4

The café. Late afternoon

Costos enters and sets up the café (See p. 60)

Helen enters and stands forlornly for a moment before sitting at her usual table

Costos comes up to her

The music fades to a lower level

Costos Whaddaya want?
Helen Er ...
Costos You have to drink, yeah?
Helen Tell me — is there any chance you'll actually bring me what I order?
Costos No. Definitely no.
Helen Then bring me whatever you like.
Costos You are a wise young lady. I know it all along.

Costos exits

The music fades up to its full level again

Helen takes out a notebook and tries to write, but she can't concentrate and ends up staring into space

The Tramp enters

The music fades

Tramp (*surprised and pleased to see Helen*) 'Allo, miss.
Helen (*surprised*) Oh, my goodness!
Tramp You look surprised to see me.
Helen Well, I suppose I am, in a way.
Tramp You shouldn't be. I'm in 'ere all the time.
Helen Well ... Maybe it's just nice to meet someone who *looks* familiar who really *is* familiar — if you see what I mean?

Tramp (*after a pause to try and work this out*) No. You've lost me there, miss. Sounds like double dutch to me.

Helen It doesn't matter.

Tramp Mind if I sit meself down? I've been on me feet all day.

Helen Oh — please.

Tramp (*sitting opposite her*) Ooh! That's better. I've been looking out for you.

Helen Have you?

Tramp I wanted to ask you.

Helen Ask me what?

Tramp 'Ow you got on, of course.

Helen Got on? What with?

Tramp With Mister "Er — er — um". What d'yer think?

Helen Oh. Yes.

Tramp I did a spell. Don't you remember?

Helen Yes. Yes, of course I do.

There is a slight pause

Tramp Well? (*Slight pause*) Did 'e turn up then?

Helen Oh, yes. He turned up all right.

Tramp Good on 'im! I must 'ave a bit of magic in me after all, then.

Helen Yes.

Tramp What was 'e like? Anything come of it?

Helen He was lovely.

Tramp (*all romantic*) Oh — that is nice.

Helen But I've left him.

Tramp What?

Helen No. Actually, he told me to go.

Tramp Oh my gawd! What's 'appened *this* time?

Helen I accused him of sleeping with his wife.

Tramp 'Is wife?

Helen Yes. Jane her name is.

Tramp (*after thinking for a moment*) I think I'm out of my depth 'ere. 'E's married, is 'e?

Helen Yes. But they've been living apart for over a year now.

Tramp (*understanding*) Oh. I get yer.

Helen He says he's madly in love with me.

Tramp Does 'e?

Helen He says he is.

Tramp Believe 'im, do yer?

Helen Well … Yes — but …

There is a slight pause

Tramp But what?

Helen Well ... It's just that the two of them seem to be taking forever to do anything about a divorce. And he's round at her house — his old house — all the time.

Tramp Is 'e?

Helen Several times a week.

Tramp Yeah ... I can see 'ow that could be a bit 'ard to take.

Helen It is.

There is a slight pause

Tramp All this ... It's got nothing to do with 'is kids, 'as it?

Helen His kids?

Tramp I bet 'e'd do anything for those kids.

Helen How do you know he has kids?

There is a slight pause

Tramp Lucky guess. (*Slight pause*) You see — maybe — in a funny kind of way — doing the legals with 'is missus means losing a bit of the kids as well.

Helen But it doesn't. Of course it doesn't. No more than he's lost already.

Tramp Do they live with 'er?

Helen Yes. They do.

Tramp That's why 'e's round there all the time, then, isn't it?

Helen Oh, yes. I know it is. Of course I know it is. (*Slight pause*) But that's a daytime thought. That's a sunny daytime thought when everything's going well and you believe everything everyone tells you. It's not a middle of the night thought, when you're lying there trying to sleep and all you can think about is her and him together in that house doing God knows what and you not there to see what's happening. (*Pause*) I can't cope with that.

Pause

Tramp Do you love 'im?

Helen (*simply*) Yes. (*Slight pause*) Yes, I do.

Tramp Seems a bit of a waste, then. For the sake of a few sleepless nights.

Helen sighs

Tramp You never know, the next one you fall for might *really* be sleeping with 'is ex-wife.

There is a slight pause

Helen What?

There is a slight pause

Tramp What?

Helen Do you know something I don't? Is there something you're not telling me?

Tramp (*with a sheepish grin*) I've given the game away a bit, haven't I?

Helen What game?

Tramp I'd better come clean, 'adn't I?

Helen I don't understand.

Tramp You remember when I saw you last time …

Helen Yes?

Tramp I was on me way to the solicitor. I don't suppose you remember.

Helen Yes, I do. To sort out *your* divorce, wasn't it?

Tramp That's right, miss. Well, I was walking towards 'is office when I saw this *Standard* lying on the pavement — somebody must've just dropped it, I suppose — the litter in this part of London is getting worse and worse — anyway, I picked it up to 'ave a quick look — just to pass the time, if yer know what I mean. I've got it 'ere with me now, miss. (*He gets the paper out of his pocket and hands it to Helen*) 'Ere. 'Ave a look yerself.

Helen (*taking the paper*) What about it?

Tramp See what the date is at the top.

Helen (*reading*) Tuesday the sixth of February.

Tramp No. The year, I mean.

Helen Nineteen-ninety-five. (*This can be altered to suit the production*)

Tramp There you are.

Helen What?

Tramp Six years ago, you see.

Pause

Helen What was it doing on the pavement, then?

Tramp I dunno. Just got missed, I suppose.

Helen For six years?

Tramp 'Ave a look at page eighteen.

Helen (*finding page eighteen*) Page eighteen?

Tramp Under "Deaths".

Helen Deaths. Oh. There's only one.

Tramp I know there is. Go on, then. Read it out.

Helen (*reading*) "Fitzpatrick, Michael, died suddenly of a heart attack January the sixteenth aged forty-seven. He leaves a widow, Audrey … " (*Breaking off suddenly*) Audrey!

Tramp Yeah. It seems she didn't so much walk out on me as I walked out on 'er! In a manner of speaking.

Helen But ... ?

Tramp The moment I saw the name I remembered it. Michael Fitzpatrick, that's me.

Helen But — you're here now — sitting here now — with *me*.

Tramp Well ... everyone 'as to 'ave their guardian angel, don't they? Eh?

Pause

Helen But ... (*Pause*) My God! They were all you.

Tramp 'Oo were?

Helen All those people we met — all those people I thought looked the same. They were all you.

Tramp Course they were! No-one else 'as got a mug as ugly as mine, now 'ave they? (*In Costos's voice*) Bloody fuse box! (*In the airport Check-in Man's voice*) Gate number seventeen, Helen! (*In the stewardess's voice*) Would you like a drink, madam? (*In the Irish Hotel Receptionist's voice*) Welcome to the Starkright hotel, Cork. (*In the American Hotel Receptionist's voice*) The elevator's right over there. (*In the Japanese Hotel Receptionist's voice*) Oh! You're English, aren't you? (*In the Russian Hotel Receptionist's voice*) Sign here, please. (*In the Pizza Delivery Man's voice*) Are you all right? (*In the Zoo-keeper's voice*) Penguins at two-thirty. Seals just before at two fifteen. (*Slight pause; in his own voice*) You never saw us together, did yer?

Helen No — never.

Tramp Look ... I've worked very 'ard on this one. Try to make a go of it, eh?

Helen Do you think I can't decide for myself?

Tramp Course you can!

Helen This is my life, you know.

Tramp I know it is. Don't stop me 'elping you out a bit, though, does it?

Helen Well ... I think it's all rather up to Jools, isn't it? He's the one who told me to go away.

Tramp If you say so, miss. Oh, by the way, talking of 'elping people out, d'you think you could spare me a week or so?

Helen Spare you?

Tramp Yeah. I'd quite like to go and spend a bit of time wiv my Audrey. She seemed a bit down when I looked in on 'er a couple of days ago. Didn't know it was me, of course. Thought I was the dustman. I'd like to try and work a little bit of magic for 'er too, if I can. She deserves a bit of a life after six years on 'er own.

Helen I don't have any claim over you — Michael.

Tramp Well ... Yes, you do, actually.

Helen Of course you must go and help Audrey.

Tramp Thanks, miss. I'll keep in touch. Just in case anything crops up.

Helen smiles

There is a slight pause

Helen Do you think Jools will want me back?
Tramp Odds on, I'd say.
Helen Always supposing I wanted to go back, of course.
Tramp Always supposing that, of course.

"I Couldn't Live Without Your Love" by Petula Clark plays

Tramp In fact, I'd say 'e'll probably be walking through that door in about
   five seconds.
Helen Five seconds?
Tramp Five or six. 'Ard to say.
Helen How do you know that?
Tramp Because I'm your bleedin' guardian angel, aren't I? I know
   everything.

*The Tramp smiles at Helen, who smiles back. She takes his hand and he
comfortingly puts his other hand over hers*

   Jools appears behind Helen

*The Tramp signals to Helen to look over her shoulder. She does, sees Jools
and returns his gaze*

   The Tramp quietly slips away and exits, unnoticed by Helen

*Helen stands up and faces Jools on the opposite side of the room. They walk
to meet each other in the middle. Jools takes Helen's hands in his. They look
into each other's eyes, then start to give each other little kisses, culminating
in a long passionate comfortable kiss. They break the kiss, smile at each
other, almost laugh with joy and relief, and then hug*

The Lights fade to black-out then come up fully

Helen and Jools bow and move to the exit US

   They bring on the Tramp from US. He sports a tiny pair of angel's wings

The Tramp comes DS *between Helen and Jools and bows*

  All three bow and exit

Petula Clark fades out

"Lift Me Up" by Geri Halliwell plays as the audience leave

FURNITURE AND PROPERTY LIST

The original Rumpus Theatre Company production was performed on a very simple set, with a plain white screen upstage, providing entrances and exits, and six large wooden boxes (four rectangular, 36 by 18 by 18 inches; 2 square, 18 by 18 by 18 inches, each with hand holes for easy carrying) which could be rearranged by the actors to make all the furniture needed on stage. The following Furniture and Property List is based on the assumption that a similar setting will be used, and that the changes to the set will be undertaken by the actors, not the Stage Management, but the author is at pains to point out that many other types of setting are possible and, indeed, to be encouraged, depending on the taste of future directors and designers and the facilities available to them.

ACT I
SCENE 1

On stage:	Boxes: two rectangles on their ends to make a gateway; one rectangle and one square laid on their sides each side of the gateway to form a low wall
Off stage:	Barely closed, badly packed suitcase; teddy, tapes, clothes, books, etc. (**Helen**)
Personal:	**Helen**: purse containing coins **Jools**: wrist-watch (worn throughout)

SCENE 2

Re-set:	Boxes: one rectangle on end with a tabletop added; two squares as chairs; other three rectangles US to form another table and two benches
Set:	*On café table*: grubby menu, ashtray, salt cellar, bottle of vinegar
Off stage:	Tea towel (**Costos**) Fish sandwich on a plate, mug of tea (**Tramp**) Chicken sandwich on a plate; cutlery and napkin (**Costos**) Glass of Coke (**Costos**) "Cyber baby" toy (**Jools**) Cheese salad, glass of milk, cutlery and napkin (**Costos**)

SCENE 3

Re-set:	Boxes: two rectangles side by side on end with two squares on top to form high check-in desk; other two rectangles form two reception seats
Set:	By check-in desk: scales On check-in desk: labels, boarding cards
Off stage:	Case (**Jools**) Overnight bag (**Helen**)
Personal:	**Jools**: tickets and passport **Helen**: passport

SCENE 4

Re-set:	Boxes: boxes laid on their sides in two rows, leaving an aisle for the Stewardess to travel down
Off stage:	Trolley (perhaps a rectangular box carried as if pushed) with drinks, glasses, etc. (**Stewardess**)
Personal:	**Jools**: money

SCENE 5

Re-set:	Boxes: reception desk, same as check-in desk in Scene 3 but on opposite side of stage; other boxes arranged as reception seats
Set:	On check-in desk: pen in holder, register, room keys

SCENE 6

Re-set:	Boxes: leave reception desk; move one rectangle from reception seating to DC, on its side

SCENE 7

Off stage:	Duvet, pillows (**Jools** and **Helen**)

After **Jools** and **Helen** move to the opposite side of the stage on page 30:

Re-set:	Boxes: leave reception desk; lay two rectangles on opposite side of stage to form a (very foreshortened) bed

SCENE 8

No additional properties

SCENE 9

No additional properties

SCENE 10

No additional properties

SCENE 11

No additional properties

SCENE 12

As "Say It Again" plays on page 33

Re-set: Boxes: dismantle reception desk; use all boxes to build bridge parapet

SCENE 13

No additional properties

ACT II
SCENE 1

On stage: Boxes: one rectangle on its side as a coffee table; sofa built out of other
              boxes

              Remote control
              Telephone
              Bottle of gin
              Glass
              Helen's bag. *In it*: purse containing ten pound note

Off stage: Pizza in box (**Pizza Delivery Man**)

After **Helen** switches on "Dancing in the Moonlight" on page 38:

Re-set: Boxes: two pillars built out of boxes

Scene 2

Off stage: Pint of beer, cocktail (**Jools**)

After **Helen**'s and **Jools**' exit on page 41

Re-set: Boxes: park bench built out of boxes

Scene 3

Off stage: Two children's backpacks (**Helen**)
                 Adult backpack containing sandwiches (**Jools**)
                 Bucket (**Zoo-keeper**)
                 Fish (**Zoo-keeper**)

Scene 4

Re-set: Boxes: as Act I, Scene 2

Off stage: Angel wings (**Tramp**)

Personal: **Helen**: notebook, pen
                 Tramp: newspaper

LIGHTING PLOT

Property fittings required: nil
Various interior and exterior settings

ACT I

To open: General exterior lighting; late afternoon in winter effect

Cue 1	**Helen** gathers her belongings and exits *Cross-fade lights to café setting; early evening*	(Page 5)
Cue 2	The music fades *Flicker lights then snap to black-out*	(Page 5)
Cue 3	**Costos**: "Bloody fuse box!" *Snap up café setting with momentary flicker*	(Page 5)
Cue 4	**Helen**: "Oh. Pot luck then." *Flicker lights then snap to black-out*	(Page 6)
Cue 5	The **Tramp** sits at the table *Snap up café setting with momentary flicker*	(Page 6)
Cue 6	**Helen**: "I'm not coming!" She looks at the door *Snap to black-out*	(Page 20)
Cue 7	**Costos**: "Bloody fuse box!" *Snap up café setting with momentary flicker*	(Page 20)
Cue 8	**Costos** exits *Cross-fade lights to Heathrow check-in lounge setting: early afternoon*	(Page 20)
Cue 9	**The Check-in Man** exits with the cases *Cross-fade lights to aeroplane interior setting*	(Page 24)
Cue 10	**Helen** and **Jools** dismantle the aeroplane *Cross-fade lights to Cork hotel reception setting*	(Page 24)
Cue 11	**Irish Receptionist** exits *Cross-fade lights to cliff setting*	(page 28)

ACT II

To open: General interior lighting; evening

EFFECTS PLOT

ACT I

Cue 30	**Jools** rolls **Helen** over *"Say It Again" by Precious*	(Page 33)
Cue 31	**Jools** and **Helen** lean on the parapet *Fade music*	(Page 33)
Cue 32	**Helen**: "No."Pause *Electronic crying*	(Page 35)
Cue 33	**Helen** hurls the toy into the river *Cut crying*	(Page 35)
Cue 34	**Jools** exits *Ship's hooter sounds*	(Page 35)

ACT II

Cue 35	To open Act II *"End of the Line" by the Honeyz*	(Page 36)
Cue 36	When ready *Decrease music volume*	(Page 36)
Cue 37	**Helen** drinks her gin *Doorbell*	(Page 36)
Cue 38	**Helen** turns down the CD player volume with the remote *Decrease volume of music*	(Page 36)
Cue 39	**Helen** turns up the CD player volume with the remote *Increase volume of music*	(Page 37)
Cue 40	**Helen** starts to eat the pizza *Phone rings*	(Page 37)
Cue 41	**Helen** turns down the CD player volume with the remote *Decrease volume of music*	(Page 37)
Cue 42	**Helen** changes the music with the remote *Cut "End of the Line"; change to "Dancing in the Moonlight"* *by Toploader, very loud*	(Page 38)
Cue 43	**Jools** and **Helen** stand about gloomily *Decrease volume volume of music very slightly*	(Page 38)
Cue 44	**Helen**: "Even to see that." *DJ announcement; change music to "Eternal Flame"* *by Atomic Kitten, slightly quieter*	(Page 39)

Cue 45	**Jools**: "Oh, definitely!"	(Page 41)
	DJ announcement; change music to "Reach for the Stars"	
	by S Club 7	
Cue 46	**Jools**: "Oh …"	(Page 41)
	Increase volume of music	
Cue 47	**Ageing Playboy** exits	(Page 41)
	Fade music	
Cue 48	Lights come up on zoo setting	(Page 41)
	Animal noises and the noises of children playing	
	in an adventure playground; continue quietly through scene	
Cue 49	**Jools**: "Come on!"	(Page 49)
	Fade animal noises; bring up "Sometimes"	
	by Britney Spears	
Cue 50	**Costos** comes up to **Helen**	(Page 50)
	Fade music to lower level	
Cue 51	**Costos** exits	(Page 50)
	Increase volume of music to full level	
Cue 52	**Tramp** enters	(Page 50)
	Fade music	
Cue 53	**Tramp**: "Always supposing that, of course."	(Page 55)
	"I Couldn't Live Without Your Love" by Petula Clark	
Cue 54	All three bow and exit	(Page 56)
	Fade Petula Clark music; bring up "Lift Me Up"	
	by Geri Halliwell	